Oxford basics
for children

VOCABULARY ACTIVITIES

Oxford Basics series

Presenting New Language
Simple Listening Activities
Simple Writing Activities
Simple Reading Activities
Simple Speaking Activities
Classroom English
Intercultural Activities
Teaching Grammar
Cross-curricular Activities

See the Oxford University Press ELT website at
http://www.oup.com/elt for further details.

Oxford basics for children

Vocabulary Activities

MARY SLATTERY

OXFORD
UNIVERSITY PRESS

OXFORD

UNIVERSITY PRESS

Great Clarendon Street, Oxford OX2 6DP

Oxford University Press is a department of the University of Oxford.
It furthers the University's objective of excellence in research, scholarship,
and education by publishing worldwide in

Oxford New York

Auckland Cape Town Dar es Salaam Hong Kong Karachi
Kuala Lumpur Madrid Melbourne Mexico City Nairobi
New Delhi Shanghai Taipei Toronto

With offices in

Argentina Austria Brazil Chile Czech Republic France Greece
Guatemala Hungary Italy Japan Poland Portugal Singapore
South Korea Switzerland Thailand Turkey Ukraine Vietnam

OXFORD and OXFORD ENGLISH are registered trade marks of
Oxford University Press in the UK and in certain other countries

ISBN 978 0 19 442195 9

Printed in China

ACKNOWLEDGEMENTS

Illustrations by: Margaret Welbank © Oxford University Press

Contents

Introduction

English is now taught in many primary schools all over the world, and children from a very early age experience an English lesson as part of their daily routine. In comparison with other age groups, however, language lessons for children from 4 to 12 combine with a great many other stages of their development.

As children are natural learners, using what we know about their development helps us, as teachers, to make full use of the many vital qualities they bring to their learning such as curiosity, energy, and spontaneity.

The vocabulary activities in this book are based on the idea that children apply many of the same skills they used for acquiring their first language when they are learning a second language. School and home situations are different, of course, but there are also many similarities. Young learners in school need to hear and see English and have the opportunity to use it when they are ready. When they make an effort to use English they need to be encouraged so that they will enjoy the experience of communicating in this new language.

Vocabulary for children from 4 to 12

The activities in this book have been divided into two sections. The first ten are intended for very young learners under the age of 7, the next fifteen for children aged between 7 and 12. However, no matter how we divide children according to their age, we know that individual children's development varies a great deal. Personality also plays a big role in the way children adapt to the changes that occur as they grow and develop. So, while remembering that each class is a set of individuals, we have to use activities that suit or can be adapted to the general stage of development of our young learners.

Up to 7

For very young learners the same processes that succeeded when they were acquiring their first language are still readily available to support them when they start English.

All young learners acquire language in a variety of ways, for example, by watching, listening, imitating, and doing things. They are constantly making sense of situations and making use of non-verbal clues. Learning at this stage is a total event.

Very young learners show a clear ability to imitate the sounds they hear quite accurately and copy the way adults speak. They acquire a lot of vocabulary very quickly and this vocabulary is often

■ incidental, which means that children absorb words and phrases when they are playing or doing other activities

- the result of interaction, when they are looking at and using objects around them and listening to you, their teacher
- remembered through repetition of patterns such as phrases and rhymes while doing actions.

For these reasons, vocabulary activities for children up to 7 that capture their total attention, such as those combined with movement or interacting with puppets or toys, are particularly successful.

From 7 to 12

As children develop they become aware of how they are learning. The more teacher talk there is while organizing, setting up, preparing, and starting the activity, the more vocabulary the children absorb. Pre-activity work done with children in this way becomes very important. It is not something that should be gone through quickly in order to get to the activity. It forms a vital part of learning vocabulary, either as phrases and chunks of language or single words.

Many activities for very young learners can be adapted to suit older children. Children from 7 to 12 will still learn very effectively using all the active techniques that were used when they were under 7. But as they develop and change they can also take a more formal approach to learning. They develop strategies of their own to help them remember and succeed.

Two components that have an enormous effect on the choice and sequencing of any set of language activities are children's starting age and the number and length of classes per week. If children of 10 have had frequent lessons since they were 4, they will have processed the methods and ways of doing many activities. They should also

- have used the four language skills of speaking, listening, reading, and writing as they developed over the years
- be ready for activities with more complex language than, for example, children who started English at 8 and had only one lesson a week.

The activities in this book

In this book each vocabulary activity is described as part of a lesson. The activities progress from those that suit very young learners who learn through play and movement to activities for young learners who can read and write and are actively involved in their own learning process. The activities are based on the following educational beliefs.

Vocabulary activities

- should be appropriate for the different stages of development of very young learners or young learners
- are more effective when children are active, enjoy what they are doing, and have a sense of ownership and involvement.

And they should also

- encourage children to listen in order to respond
- allow for individual attention
- offer the opportunity to develop children's confidence
- make use of realia (real objects) and visuals – from inside or outside the classroom
- offer variety in the use of the four language skills.

How each unit is organized

Each of the units that follow describes a vocabulary activity under these headings:

Language – tells you what language is the focus of the activity, for example, parts of the body, phrases of position, etc.

Resources and preparation – lists what materials and resources you need to bring to your class for this activity and what materials and/or language preparation you might have to do.

Time guide – gives you some guidance as to how long this activity could take.

Activity – gives a description of the activity in stages and examples of teacher talk that you could use with the learners.

Variations – show you how you could use the same activity with other vocabulary items or offers you other suggestions for varying the activity.

Pronunciation – highlights features such as word stress and particular English sounds that are a problem for some leaners.

Follow-up suggestion – gives ideas for activities you could do after each vocabulary activity.

Language

Specific words, phrases, or rhymes are used as sample vocabulary in each unit. They were selected because they link with the kind of topic vocabulary you come across in coursebooks, and when you are talking about the classroom, the home, the natural world, and children's stories.

It is important to remember that children naturally absorb words and phrases from all the English you use. Everything you say in

English during a lesson is valuable exposure to language for the listening child, for example:

- instructions that look for an immediate response: *You can put your cards here on the floor…, Hold the bowl …,* and so on.
- explanations that tell your learners what you are doing and/or going to do: *I'll put it here …, We're going to have a meal …*
- phrases you use to:
  —show inclusion: *Let's work in teams …*
  —encourage co-operation: *So you can help one another …*
  —give praise: *Good … you're right …*
- descriptions of items in the classroom that children can see and handle: *We have some water in this jug …, It's small and red and round …*
- descriptions of places and people that children can see in pictures: *Here's a picture of a mouse on a table …, This animal jumps like this …*
- questions that look for different responses: *Will you hold this? Is he happy? What do you say first?*
- rhymes that children say as part of a routine when starting activities or doing actions: *What do I spy …?*

Resources and preparation

Resources can be built up over time from a variety of materials. Realia are always a great vocabulary support and many teachers use real objects that are in the classroom or bring in extra material such as clothes, food, toys, and things that children will know from the world of nature. But as you cannot have everything you want to talk about in your classroom, good visual materials, which link with the world children know or can easily imagine, are very valuable. Some of the most useful resources used in the activities in this book are visuals such as picture cards or flashcards, posters, and picture storybooks. These all provide immediate memory association and constantly support the recall of words and phrases.

Picture cards, flashcards, and posters
When introducing new vocabulary to learners, a picture of a single object or action can help make the meaning clear. A picture with one clear image makes a direct association for a learner. Pictures with lots of detail are very useful when recycling vocabulary that learners are already familiar with.

You can produce your own picture cards and/or posters by making drawings similar to the ones in coursebooks or resource books, or by cutting out pictures or photos from magazines. You can make

- picture cards by sticking drawings or photos onto cards
- cut-outs by cutting out the shape of the object you have drawn.

For example, if you cut out the shapes of fruits or clothes (like the ones on this page), you have an instant activity that children love – show them the back of a cut out and have them guess what the shape is before turning it around.

If you are preparing picture cards, you may want to add single names or phrases. Even before children are formally reading they will often recognize whole words or phrases and correctly associate them with an object or action. If you write the word on one side of a card and have the picture on the other (see the sample card 'a house'), you can cut the card at a later stage and use the two halves for matching activities.

Posters in your classroom are an ever-present reminder for children. Just as with sets of picture cards, posters can vary in shape. A poster for fruit could be cut in the shape of a tree and a poster for furniture could be in a house shape. You can think of other ways of displaying visuals in real contexts such as clothes hung along a string with paper clips or clothes pegs.

Puppets

Puppets can be used with all young learners. Children of 4 and 5 see a puppet as real. They are fascinated by everything that the puppet does and they want to know about everything that the puppet has. This gives you the opportunity to introduce a whole range of basic vocabulary including lots of actions and descriptions from the puppet's 'life'. Because the puppet's possessions are small, children can handle them easily which is ideal for this early stage of development where so much learning is 'hand-to-head' learning. Holding something or minding something for the puppet makes very young children feel helpful and 'grown-up' and allows them to enjoy a feeling of responsibility and self-confidence. And all the time they are absorbing a new English word or phrase that you are repeating spontaneously and naturally.

Texts and stories

Picture storybooks are seen by most teachers today as an effective way to combine children's obvious enjoyment of stories and contextualized vocabulary. The illustrations, just like picture cards, help to clarify and establish meaning. You help children to remember when you use picture cards as a cue. In the same way, rereading and retelling a story offers a repeated context so memory is supported and strengthened with each contact.

In Unit 25 there is a selection of vocabulary activities you can use with a story. The suggestions offered here in two lessons can be used over several lessons. If you are telling a story with your own drawings, you can add things to talk about with your learners. Doing your own drawings means that you can revise a lot of vocabulary your learners are familiar with.

Children's imaginations are a constant source of material. Your learners can add to the details in a story through their own drawings and paintings. For example, in the sample story in Unit 25 some characters are mentioned but with very few details. Your learners could draw and talk about these characters, their homes, families, and feelings. In this way children add the details that are of interest to them and recall or learn new vocabulary. When they retell the story they can talk about their own additions and become storytellers!

You and your learners

You and your learners are the greatest resources in the classroom. In this special environment you can support the English you are using in a variety of creative ways. Miming, acting out, and using gestures and movements all reinforce meaning very effectively. Your learners can do the same to show their understanding.

Children can also make material for their own immediate use and for future learners. When they do this through English it offers the opportunity to develop language skills through listening to instructions and repeating words and phrases. At the same time they are developing

- automony and a sense of ownership through involvement in their own learning
- a sense of personal worth as they see their work and creativity valued.

Time guide

The timing of any activity will vary depending on many factors:

- the number of children in the class
- the age of the children and their general development
- whether or not your learners have done a similar activity before
- the material you are using. This may be simpler or more complex than the sample in the activity.

In most of the units the time given is what was seen as the minimum necessary.

Activity

This section is the central part of each unit. It offers you an outline of how each activity can be used in class. You can adapt or change this outline to suit your particular circumstances.

Different stages of the activity indicate how you can

- organize your learners
- give instructions and tell your class what is happening and what is going to happen
- use the resources and materials for the activity
- ask the children questions, get them to take turns, respond to their efforts, and in general interact.

Teacher talk

In each unit there are examples of the kind of teacher talk you could use in the activity. Here is an example from Unit 2:

Ask the children to make a circle and sit down. Take out the bag with the puppet inside. Show them the top of the puppet's head and let them guess who it is. Ask the children to say 'Hello'.

Now everyone hold hands … Let's make a big circle … very good … Now let's all sit down … Okay … I have a friend here who wants to say hello …

These are suggestions which you can adapt to your own situation. How you speak to your class is a personal decision for every teacher. Children usually like to talk and in their English lessons they will spontaneously comment or check with you in their mother tongue. This is because children need to feel secure and know that they are understood. How you respond, whether you answer in mother tongue or in English, depends on many factors, for example:

- the age of the children
- their experiences with English so far
- how long you have been teaching the class
- how much English you are happy to use during your lesson.

The final objective for most language teachers is to use as much English as possible during their lessons. But you can prepare to do this slowly, introducing a little more each time you are with a class. There are many times when using your learners' mother tongue is necessary and useful. However, you also want to show young learners that they can easily communicate in either language and your 'teacher talk' is an indicator to them that English is the focus in your lesson time.

Above all we want to create a relaxed and pleasant atmosphere during an English lesson. This will help children enjoy the learning experience and create a positive attitude that will remain with them.

Variations

In this section there are suggestions for adapting and extending activities so that you can use them for other vocabulary areas or for other purposes.

When children become familiar with an activity they become more confident. You can then vary the material you use and because children know how to 'do' the activity they will focus more on the language.

Pronunciation

The correct pronunciation of English sounds and word stress are both important. This section offers support to you as a teacher. The points looked at come from the language in the activity, for example:

Practise the sound /tʃ/ in words like 'stretch' and 'march'.

Stress is marked with upper case letters in words and phrases, for example:

Let's CHECK your SPELLing.

Stress can vary in English depending on emphasis. The stress given here in these examples is based on the meaning in the 'teacher talk' section of each unit.

Young learners find it easy to remember chunks of language. They have a great facility for imitation and will acquire your pronunciation and intonation patterns by listening to you.

A good dictionary is important for a teacher to check the normal stress pattern in a word. In this book I use the *Oxford Basic English Dictionary* as a resource for clear definitions and pronunciation.

Follow-up suggestions

As many vocabulary activities are short they form part of a lesson. In the follow-up sections there are suggestions on how to

- use the vocabulary in another activity
- use the activity to revise other vocabulary items
- give children a different activity altogether.

Copiable materials in the Appendix

The material in the appendix accompanies specific units. The sample material is intended as a guideline that can be copied or adapted to suit your particular needs.

Conclusion

I hope you enjoy using and adapting the activities in this book. Above all I wish you and your young learners pleasant and rewarding experiences in your English lessons.

Activities

1 What's your name?

LANGUAGE **What's your name?**
Hello [name].
Roll the ball, Catch the ball
Rhyme: '[name] has the ball.'

RESOURCES AND PREPARATION A big soft ball (bought or made) and a class toy or puppet.

A space inside or outside the classroom for all the children to make a circle.

TIME GUIDE 10 minutes.

Activity

1 Show the class how to make a big circle. Ask all the children to make a line and hold hands. Then ask the two children at the two ends of the line to hold hands. When they are standing in a circle let them clap their hands. Show them the ball and roll it to several children to practise rolling and catching.

Okay everyone let's all hold hands and now [name the last two children in the line] *Ana and Daranee … hold hands … okay … very good … Now we're in a big circle … Now everyone clap hands … clap hands … very good … Now look what I've got … a big ball … Okay now … I'm going to roll the ball … Can you catch it? … Very good … Now roll it back to me and I'll catch it … now … I'll roll it to …*

2 Let the children see a class puppet or toy they know well. Ask them who it is and ask the toy or puppet 'What's your name?' Do this a few times saying the name after you ask the question.

3 Now put the puppet between two of the children in the circle. Roll the ball to the puppet and say, 'What's your name?' Say 'Hello' and the puppet's name, for example, my puppet is a bear so I say 'Hello Bear'. Let the children repeat this and put the puppet in the middle of the circle with the ball. Sing or say the rhyme. Everyone holds hands and moves around Bear.

16

Bear has the ball – Bear has the ball – hey ho around we go – Bear has the ball.

4 When you finish the song everyone claps hands again. Use the puppet to roll the ball to a confident child and ask, 'What's your name?' Help the child to respond and repeat with all the children, 'Hello Lara'.

5 Lara stands in the middle of the circle and holds the ball. The children move around and sing the rhyme again.

Lara has the ball – Lara has the ball – hey ho around we go – Lara has the ball.

6 Lara then rolls the ball to another child and so on. Continue until everyone in the class has had the ball.

7 To finish the game pass the ball quickly from one child to the other asking 'What's your name?' and all together say 'Hello' to each child. Finally, give the ball to the puppet again and everyone sings, 'Bear has the ball', etc.

Variation

Let the children pass a shaker or a tambourine (or anything that can make music or a sound) around the circle. Say the rhyme in this unit using the words 'Who has the shaker?' When you stop singing, the child who is holding the shaker moves into the middle. The rest of the class hold hands and dance around. They say the rhyme using the child's name and the instrument, for example, 'Ana has the shaker.'

Pronunciation

Practise these phrases:

Let's HOLD HANDS
Let's MAKE a CIRcle
EVeryone ... CLAP HANDS
ROLL the BALL
CATCH the BALL
[NAME] HAS the BALL
HEY HO aROUND we GO

Remember **everyone** is said with three syllables /evriwʌn/.

Follow-up suggestion

Let children do something quietly on their own. Each child could draw a picture of himself/herself with the ball. When they finish you can write the child's name under his/her drawing and put it on the wall.

2 Puppet's bag

LANGUAGE   Puppet's possessions: **a cup, a bowl, a spoon, a blanket, a pillow, a book, two socks, a hat, some coloured pencils, a picture.**

Phrases: **here, over there, Hold this for Bear.**

RESOURCES AND PREPARATION   Use your class puppet and a bag with some things that the puppet has. My puppet, Bear, has all the items listed above. Make sure you have one object for each child.

TIME GUIDE   10–15 minutes.

Activity

1 Ask the children to make a circle and sit down. Take out the bag with the puppet inside. Show them the top of the puppet's head and let them guess who it is. Ask the children to say 'Hello'.

Now everyone hold hands … Let's make a big circle … very good … Now let's all sit down … Okay … I have a friend here who wants to say hello … Do you know who it is? Is it Hiro? … No, it's not … He's over there … Is it Mari? … No… she's here … Who is it? … Oh look … something's moving … Who is it? … Do you know who it is? It's … it's Bear … say 'Hello Bear' …

2 The object of this activity is to help the children remember the names of everything that Bear has in his bag. Talk to the children about what Bear takes out of his bag.

> *Okay … now this is Bear's bag … What's in your bag Bear? … Let's see …*

Ask a different child to hold something every time you take an object out. Make sure every child has something to hold.

> *Oh look at this … Is this your cup, Bear? It's very small but just right for you … Okay … Hiro will you hold Bear's cup? … Now let's see … What else do you have, Bear? Oh your blanket … It's lovely and warm … and it's a blue blanket … Now Mari will you hold Bear's blanket? …*

3 When everything has been taken out of the bag, you can count all the things that Bear has. Then ask the children to give the items back to Bear. Hold Bear close to your ear and pretend he is whispering to you and telling you what he wants.

> *Now let's help Bear put everything back in his bag. Okay … Now Bear what do you want to put in first? … Your blanket … okay … Who has Bear's blanket? … Mari can you give Bear his blanket? … Thank you … good … Bear, what do you want now? …*

Variations

Let the puppet have any objects you want to focus on in class:

- food the children are familiar with
- cards and decorations for special days or festivals
- things that children see at home or at school, for example, paintbrushes, markers, plates, etc.

Pronunciation

Practise asking questions:

> **What ELSE do you HAVE?**
> **[Name] will you HOLD THIS?**
> **Can you GIVE THIS to BEAR?**

Lots of common English words begin with two consonantal sounds like *sp*oon and *bl*anket. Practise the sounds at the beginning of words, for example: **spell, speak, spot, spill,** and **black, blue, blow.**

Follow-up suggestion

Let the children take everything out of their bags to show to Bear.

3 A colour tree

LANGUAGE

Colours: **red, yellow, blue, green, pink, brown, orange, purple, white, black.**

Phrases: **in his hand, in her hand, in your hand, in my hand.**
Rhyme: 'Colour tree'.

RESOURCES AND PREPARATION

Decide what colours you want to use. There are ten in this sample lesson.

Use a leaf shape and cut out 30 leaves (three sets of 10).

Use colour card, or colour the leaves when you have cut them out. Put sticky tape on the backs of the cards.

Keep one set of leaves so that you can say and show the colours to the children.

Draw a big tree shape on a big piece of cardboard.

Put coloured spots on the tree shape so that children can see where to stick their leaves.

TIME GUIDE

15 minutes.

Activity

1 Remind the children about leaves and trees by showing them real leaves from trees or some pictures.

2 Show the children your sets of coloured leaves. Explain that you are going to make a 'colour tree'.

Let's make a colour tree for our classroom. Okay … let's put the tree up here. Now this tree doesn't have any leaves but I have some here in this box. Can you see them? They are all different colours. Let's see … this one is … yellow … a yellow leaf … Who wants a yellow leaf? … Okay … Ana here's a yellow leaf for you … Ana has a yellow leaf …

3 Give a leaf to each child and sing or say this rhyme.

Ana has a yellow leaf … a yellow leaf … a yellow leaf
Ana has a yellow leaf
In her hand …

Now this leaf is red … a red leaf … Who wants a red leaf? … Okay … Juan here's a red leaf for you … Juan has a red leaf … so let's say our rhyme.

Juan has a red leaf … a red leaf … a red leaf
Juan has a red leaf
In his hand …

4 When each child has a leaf show them how to stick a leaf on the tree.

Now I have an orange leaf and I can stick my leaf on the colour tree … Where will I put it? … Can you see the colour orange on the tree? … Yes … there's an orange spot … Okay so I'm going to stick my orange leaf on the tree … right here … beside the spot … like this … Now it's on the tree … Okay … who has a yellow leaf … like this spot? … Who has this colour? …

5 Let the children do this one by one and then sing or say the rhyme.

Now we have a colour tree, a colour tree, a colour tree
Now we have a colour tree
In our room.

Variations

1 Cut out fruit shapes and use them instead of leaves.

2 Let the children draw outlines of their hands and colour them. You can write their names on these outlines before asking the children to stick them on a tree shape. This can be the class friendship tree.

Pronunciation

Remember the stress pattern for these chunks in the rhyme:

Ana has a YELLow LEAF

Juan has a RED LEAF

Follow-up suggestion

Take the leaves off the tree one by one and let the children find things in the classroom with the same colours.

21

4 Puppet's book

<table>
<tr><td>LANGUAGE</td><td>Food and drink: apple, banana, mango, pasta, watermelon, beans, rice, cheese, plum, bread, egg, orange juice, ice cream, pear, jam.</td></tr>
</table>

RESOURCES AND PREPARATION — Make a book for your class puppet like this:

- Make a hard cover with strong material such as cardboard.
- Cut out pieces of card the same size.
- Tie the pieces of card into the cover with string like the drawing on this page.

- Collect a set of photos of food and drink from magazines, etc. or draw simple pictures.
- Stick the photos and drawings on the pieces of card. If you can cover them, they will last longer.
- Write the names of the food or drink under the photos.

TIME GUIDE — 15 minutes.

Activity

1 The object of this activity is to help the children remember the names of the food and drink in the puppet's book. Let the children make a circle and sit down.

2 Talk about the puppet's book and ask the children if they would like to read the puppet's book with him.

Bear is reading a big book. Do you want to read it? Let's ask Bear. Bear … Bear can we read your book with you? Yes … good … okay … Let's look at Bear's book.

3   Show the children the pictures in the book. Ask the class if they like the food on each page. Take the picture off the page and give it to the child who says 'Yes!'

Look … Bear's book is all about what Bear likes to eat and drink … On this page there's a banana. Who likes bananas? Wei … Good … so Wei will you hold this picture for Bear … good … Now let's see … on this page there's some rice … Bear loves rice … Do you like rice? Who likes rice? Okay … Hong … very good … Will you hold this picture for Bear? …

4   Take the pictures out of the book and give one to each child. Ask the children to show Bear the different pictures.

Show Bear a mango.

5   Talk to the puppet and ask him what he likes.

Do you like rice Bear?

6   Ask the children to help Bear put the photos back in the book again.

Who has Bear's banana? … Okay, let's give it back to Bear.

If the children can't remember, help them and say the name with them.

Variations

1   Use the puppet's book to introduce and use vocabulary for family, home, animals, transport, places, etc.

2   Use other photos or drawings that the children can identify with.

Pronunciation

Let's is a useful phrase when you want children to do something with you:

Let's ASK … let's SEE … let's LOOK at …

Practise the sound /ʤ/ in the words: **juice**, **jam**, and **orange**.

Follow-up suggestion

Show the children how to make a class book of their favourite things. Let them choose what to put in the book and tell them the names in English. Write the names under the photos or drawings.

5 Point to ...

LANGUAGE Transport: **car, truck, plane, train, bike, bus.** You can use any other kind of transport that your children are familiar with.

Colours: **yellow, blue, red, green.**

Rhyme: 'Point to' (see the 'Pronunciation' section).

RESOURCES AND PREPARATION Draw a car, a truck, a plane, a train, a bike, and a bus on coloured paper or card. If they are on coloured paper, stick them on card to make them stronger.

Make coloured sets of these six types of transport so you have a blue set, a red set, etc.

Keep them in different boxes or envelopes.

TIME GUIDE 15 minutes.

Activity

1 Ask the children to sit in a circle.

2 Show them one set of cards and talk about them.

Now what's in this envelope? ... This is a car ... What colour is it? ... Yes, Takeshi ... Yes ... it's yellow ... good ... It's a yellow car ... beep, beep, beep ... Now let's see what else we have ...

3 Show the children the other vehicles and do an action or make a sound for each of them.

4 Give one set to each group of six children. Tell them to put the sets on the floor.

Okay let's put the cards on the floor ... What have you got in your envelope? ... You've got a blue bike and a blue truck ... You can put your cards here on the floor ...

And ... what have you got over here? ... You've got a red car and a red truck ...

5 Ask the children to point to the different items on the floor, for example, a red car, a green car, a blue truck, a yellow truck, etc.

Okay ... Chie ... show me a green plane ... Yes, very good ... a green plane.

6 Ask the children to put all the cards in a big circle, one after the other. Let the children form a circle outside the cards. Play some music or sing a song or say a rhyme (see the 'Pronunciation' section). Let the children dance around until the music stops, or you finish the rhyme or song.

7 Now ask different children to point to something that is near them.

Okay Saori ... point to a yellow plane ... Very good ... and Hiro point to a green bus ... Okay ... very good ... and ...

8 When you finish let the children tidy up and put all the sets back in envelopes and put them away in the cupboard.

Variations

1 Use other vocabulary sets, for example, furniture, shapes.

2 Use this rhyme when the children are doing the activity:

POINT to a BUS
POINT to a TRAIN
POINT to a LITtle CAR
Now POINT to a PLANE

POINT to a TRUCK
POINT to a BIKE
POINT to a LITtle CAR
THAT'S the ONE I LIKE.

Pronunciation

Plane /pleɪn/ and **train** /treɪn/ are spelt differently but they have the same vowel sound.

Practise the consonant clusters 'pl' and 'tr'. They are in lots of words you will use, for example:

'pl' – **place, planet, plant, plastic, plate, play, playground, please.**

'tr' – **traffic, treasure, tree, trousers, try.**

Follow-up suggestion

Let each child draw his/her favourite vehicle and colour it.

6 A tidy-up rhyme

LANGUAGE Phrases you want your children to be familiar with for tidying up.

The rhyme in this unit is adapted from an old English rhyme. You can sing it or say it.

This is the way I tidy my desk
Tidy my desk, tidy my desk
This is the way I tidy my desk
Everyday in our classroom.

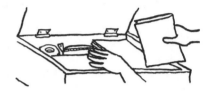

This is the way I collect the pencils
Collect the pencils, collect the pencils
This is the way I collect the pencils
And put them all away.

This is the way I hang up my painting
Hang up my painting, hang up my painting
This is the way I hang up my painting
And stick it on the wall.

This is the way I pick up paper
Pick up paper, pick up paper
This is the way I pick up paper
And put it in the bin.

This is the way I take a rest
Take a rest, take a rest
This is the way I take a rest
When all the work's been done.

RESOURCES AND PREPARATION Think about how your learners help you tidy up in the classroom.

You can prepare new phrases and add them to the rhyme. Each verse of the rhyme starts with 'This is the way'.

Start with one or two verses and add more over the school year.

TIME GUIDE 10 minutes.

Activity

1   Let the children stand in a circle and ask everyone to look around the room. Tell them you're going to tidy the room and ask them to help.

Okay everyone … our room is very untidy … very messy. Let's tidy it and we can say a tidy up rhyme … Okay … first of all … we're going to tidy our desks/tables … so we say:

This is the way I tidy my desk
Tidy my desk, tidy my desk
This is the way I tidy my desk
Everyday in our classroom.

2   When you say a new part of the rhyme, do the activity yourself, for example, tidy your desk while you are saying the rhyme. Then let the children go to their desks and tidy them. Say the rhyme again with the children.

3   Follow the pattern in stage 2 for all the actions that you want to do. This last verse can be used to praise the children's work.

And this is what my teacher says
My teacher says, my teacher says
And this is what my teacher says
Very good … well done … well done!

Variation

Use the rhyme for other kinds of actions, for example, movements: 'This is the way we jump up and down / everyday in the playground.' 'Stand very still …', etc.

Pronunciation

These syllables are stressed in the rhyme:

TIdy my DESK / EVery DAY in our CLASSroom
coLLECT the PENcils or MARkers or CRAyons / PUT them ALL aWAY
PICK up PAper or RUBbish / And PUT it in the BIN
HANG up my PAINTing/ And STICK it on the WALL
TAKE a REST /When ALL the WORK has been DONE.

Follow-up suggestion

Show the children simple line drawings of tidy-up activities like the sample ones above and name all the activities. Let the children colour them and talk about them.

You could put them in a sequence and stick them on the wall where the children can see them as a reminder.

7 Making dough – just so!

Ingredients: **some water, some flour, some salt, some oil.**

Making the dough: **shake the sieve, stir it slowly, add the water, mix it all together, squeeze them together, roll it around.**

RESOURCES AND PREPARATION You need a big bowl, a sieve, a cup, a spoon, and the ingredients in the recipe.

Use containers that hold the amount you need.

Practise making some dough and bring it to class in case something goes wrong!

Recipe
Dry ingredients
3 cups of flour – 400 grams
1 cup of salt – 200 grams

Wet ingredients
1¼ cups of water – 200 millilitres
2 large spoons of oil – 10 millilitres
Food colouring – a few drops.

Put the dry ingredients together.
Put all the wet ingredients together.
Mix everything and roll into a ball.

TIME GUIDE 15–20 minutes.

....

Activity

1 Tell the children that you want them to help you make some play dough. Show them what you are going to use.

   Now everyone look at what we have on the table … We have some water … in this jug … and some flour in this yellow box … Look how soft it is … and some salt in this blue box … and some oil in this bottle … and some food colouring in this little bottle … Can you see what colour it is? It's … it's pink, isn't it? … Now I want you to help me …

2 Show the children the containers you are going to use. Give each child something to hold.

> *Now I need a lot of help … Will you help me? … Okay … very good … Now we have a very big bowl … Can you stand beside the bowl Clara? … and make sure nothing spills … Let's see … Margo and Raul can you hold the sieve? … Thank you … can you hold this cup? … good … and …*

3 Let each child come forward to fill their cup or container with some of the ingredients and put it in the sieve or the bowl.

> *Okay … now Clara hold the bowl and Raul hold the sieve over the bowl … very good … Now, Ana here's some flour … Hold the cup carefully and fill it with flour … very good … Now you can put your flour into the sieve and Raul you have to shake it … shake the sieve … very carefully … into the bowl … Very good … well done … now Margo … stir the flour slowly … Isabel you're going to add some water … very good …*

4 When each child has added something let them help mix the dough into one big ball. Take it out. Divide it up into smaller balls. Count each one as you give them to the children.

> *Will you all help me mix it together? … Now we have to squeeze everything together … very good … and … roll it around … and let's make some small balls … one for everyone …*

5 Let the children make whatever they like with their ball of dough. Let them use cutter shapes. Talk to them about what they make.

Variation

Make other simple things that your learners can all eat. For example, let them help prepare a fruit salad by holding the fruit and counting the pieces you put in the bowl, etc.

Pronunciation

Practise the stress in these phrases and notice the reduced stress for 'some' /ə/.

> **some WATer … and some FLOUR … and some SALT and some OIL … and some FOOD COLouring.**

Follow-up suggestion

Let all the children help with tidying up and sing your 'Tidy-up' song.

8 A movement rhyme

LANGUAGE Action words, for example: **walk/walking, shake hands/shaking hands, march/marching, wiggle/wiggling, curl up/curling up, stretch/stretching, jump/jumping, climb/climbing, hop/hopping, dance/dancing, fly/flying, skip/skipping.**

You can start with four or five actions and add more as the children become more familiar with them.

RESOURCES AND PREPARATION Practise any actions you want the children to do. Think about where the children will do the actions. You will need plenty of space. Start with slow movements then do some fast movements and finish with slow movements. This allows the children's muscles to warm up and then cool down. In this way they use up excess energy and calm down before another activity.

TIME GUIDE 10 minutes.

Activity

1 Ask the children to make a big circle in the classroom or outside. Make sure there is plenty of space.

Okay everyone let's hold hands and make a big circle … Everyone ready? …

2 When the children are in a circle say the rhyming lines and do the first action.

Now let's see … let's do some actions … First of all let's go for a walk around the classroom (playground) … Follow me … let's walk slowly first and … say a rhyme.

(Walk around in a circle while you say the rhyme.)

I like walking
I like walking, walking, walking
I like walking
One two three
I like walking, walking, walking
I like walking
Walk with me.

Now let's walk very slowly … now walk quickly … Good … Now let's …

3 When you walk slowly, say the words slowly and when you walk quickly, say the words quickly.

4 Do several actions such as walking slowly and quickly, wiggling all over, curling up, and so on before you do some stretching actions. Each time you do a new action say the rhyme changing the action words to suit, for example, 'I like stretching …', 'I like skipping …', etc.

Variation

Use any miming actions that your learners would enjoy such as imitating different animals and birds. Change the rhyme to suit.

Pronunciation

Practise the 'ch' sound /tʃ/ in **mar*ch*** and **stret*ch***. This is two sounds /t/ and /ʃ/. Practise by making the sound /t/ then make the sound /ʃ/. Repeat them more quickly each time you say them. Soon you will be saying the sound /tʃ/. It is a short sound.

Remember the silent letters in **wa*l*k** and **cli*m*b**.

Follow-up suggestion

Do a quiet activity like reading a story.

9 What's in the bag?

LANGUAGE Names of animals the children already know.

Rhyme: 'What's in the bag?'

RESOURCES AND PREPARATION You need:

■ a cloth bag or a pillowcase

■ pictures of animals, birds, or insects that children can mime and make sounds for: duck, monkey, elephant, bird, kangaroo, lion, spider, frog, rabbit, dog, cat.

TIME GUIDE 10–15 minutes.

Activity

1 Let the children make a circle and sit down. Tell them the puppet wants to play a game.

   Now Bear wants to play a game … a guessing game.

2 Show the children the bag. Tell them that the puppet has lots of pictures of animals in his bag.

3 Say the rhyme and encourage the children to clap out the rhythm.

   What's in the bag?
   What's in the bag?
   Is it a dog?
   Is it a cat?
   I don't know
   About that!
   What's in the bag?
   What's in the bag?

4 Now tell the children what they are going to do and show them by doing it yourself.

   I'm going to take a picture out of the bag … now … Let me see … no looking … okay … This animal doesn't walk … This animal jumps like this … jumping … jumping … jumping like a … Can you guess? … Yes … you're right … I'm a kangaroo … very good … Now who wants to take a picture? Okay … Cristina …

5 Let each child take a picture from the bag, and move or make a sound like the animal in the picture. The other children should try to guess the animal. The children keep their picture beside them until everyone finishes.

6 At the end of the activity ask each child to put his/her picture in the puppet's bag.

   Okay … who has the duck? … quack … quack … good Marco … Can you put it in the bag please? …

Variations

1 Use pictures of people who make obvious movements while they work: a policeman directing traffic, a bus driver, and so on.

2 Use pictures of clothes and let the children act out how they put them on.

Pronunciation

You can talk about what the children are doing when they are miming the animals or saying the sounds. Remember the 'ng' sound /ŋ/ is made through your nose. For example:

> WALKing on TWO BIG FEET … SAYing 'QUACK QUACK' (Duck)
> has a VEry LONG NOSE … MOVing SLOWly (Elephant)
> FLYing aROUND … USing his /her ARMS like WINGS (Bird)
> ROARing … WALKing aROUND on FOUR LEGS (Lion)
> HOPPing aROUND… SAYing 'RIBBIT' (Frog).

Animals make the same sounds but in language we express them differently. In English, animals make the following sounds:

bees	bzzz	hens	cluck
birds	tweet	horses	neigh
cats	meow	lions	roar
cows	moo	mice	squeak
dogs	woof / bow wow	pigs	oink
donkeys	hee-haw	roosters	cock a doodle doo
ducks	quack	sheep	baa
frogs	ribbit/croak		

Follow-up suggestion

Read a story about animals or look at pictures of animals and talk about them.

10 A body rhyme

LANGUAGE Parts of the body.

Phrases used in the rhyme.

RESOURCES AND PREPARATION Read the body rhyme and decide what actions you will use with each part.

TIME GUIDE 10 minutes.

Activity

1 Choose a part of your classroom with enough space for actions, or go outside.

2 Ask all the children to do the actions with you while you say the rhyme. For example,

These are my hands,
This is me.
Come out and play,
One, two, three.

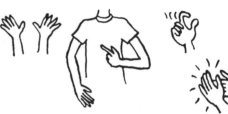

These are my legs,
These are my feet.
This is how
I hop along the street.

These are my arms,
These are my knees.
This is how
I fly like the bees.

This is my neck,
This is my head.
This is how
I go to bed.

This is my face,
This is my hair.
Look, I'm dancing
Like a bear.

These are my eyes,
This is my nose.
Now look down,
these are my toes.

These are my ears
This is mouth
Listen to me
I can shout!!

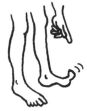

Wow Wow Wow

Now you know
I'm just like you.
Come and see
What we can do!

Variation

Help your learners to do this rhyme as a class performance. Give each pair two lines to say. Let them practise using dramatic gestures.

Pronunciation

Practise the stress pattern in phrases with **this** and **these**.

THESE are my EYES, THIS is my NOSE …

Make sure children say the same final sound /k/ in **stomach, back, neck,** and **Jack**.

Follow-up suggestion

Let the children draw some pictures of themselves doing the actions.

11 Say it and pass it on

LANGUAGE   Items which learners might see or use outside the classroom, for example: **mirror, bowl, towel, torch, comb, envelope, map, postcard, stamp, key.**

RESOURCES AND PREPARATION   Prepare sets of ten pictures of objects that you want to introduce.

For a small class you could use realia but for a class of more than 20 learners, prepare two sets of the same ten pictures. If you have a very big class (30 to 40) you will need three or four sets of cards.

TIME GUIDE   15–20 minutes.

Activity

1   Introduce the ten new words by showing your learners the picture cards. Show them three or four pictures at a time and say what each one is. Repeat some of the earlier words at intervals to help them remember all ten.

> *Now I'm going to show you some pictures and I want you to repeat the names after me ... so ... This is ... a mirror ... Now you say it ... a mirror ... very good ... a mirror ... Let's put it here ... a mirror ... And this is a bowl ... a bowl* [learners repeat] *very good.*

2   Let them help you put the pictures on the board so that everyone can see them.

> *... Li ... please put the bowl beside the mirror ... thank you ... and this is a towel ... a towel ...* [learners repeat] *very good ... so ... a mirror ... a bowl ... and a towel ...*

3   When you have said all ten words call out different objects and ask learners in groups to point to the cards.

> *Can you all see the cards on the board? ... Okay ... Can you remember some of the names? ... Let's work in groups ... so you can help one another ... Ming and Yun and Li ... point to the torch ... the torch ... yes ... good ... That's the torch ...*

4   Now collect the picture cards. Tell your learners that you are going to play a repetition game. Ask your learners to sit or stand in a circle.

5 Hold up the first card and say, 'Here's a torch'. Pass the card to the learner beside you.

6 Ask the learners to repeat, 'Here's a torch'. They have to pass the card on to the next learner who has to say the same phrase 'Here's a torch'. Everyone in the circle has to repeat the phrase when they get the picture.

7 When the first card has gone to three learners then give the first learner another card saying, for example, 'Here's a bowl' and let them repeat it. When this card is at the third learner pick up another card and send it around. Listen carefully for any pronunciation and stress difficulties.

8 When the first card comes back to you hold it until the last card has been given out. Then repeat all the cards again but change the order.

Variations

Use this activity:

- to practise phrases like, 'This is my … this is your … this is our …'
- to practise counting, for example, 'I have four apples … I have some rice …'
- for action pictures and phrases, for example, 'I like running …' or 'I like table tennis'.
  You can make the activity into a fun game by sending the pictures around in both directions!

Pronunciation

Practise the stress in:

POSTcard, ENvelope, and MIRRor.

Remember:

- the letter 'b' is not pronounced in the word **comb**
- **envelope**, **stamp** and **map** all end in the sound /p/
- the pronunciation of 'ow' in **bowl** /oʊ/ and **towel** /aʊ/ is different.

Follow-up suggestion

Do an activity such as 'What's Missing' (Unit 12) with the same vocabulary set.

12 What's missing?

LANGUAGE
A group of items connected with a place or situation, for example, things on a table at mealtimes: **a knife, a fork, a spoon, a bowl, chopsticks, a plate, a glass, a cup and saucer, a jug of water.**

Phrases to show position: **beside, in front of, near.**

Instructions: **Turn round, Don't look, No looking, Take something away, You can look now, Put something back.**

RESOURCES AND PREPARATION   Real things or picture cards for each item.

TIME GUIDE   10–15 minutes.

Activity

1 Put all the items or picture cards where your learners can see them, for example, on a table or on the board. Explain the situation.

   Now ... we are going to have a meal ... and we need all these things ... I want you to repeat the names after me.

2 Show and say the name of the objects or the picture cards. Let the children repeat each one.

   This is a knife ... say it everyone ... very good ... Let's put the knife here ... a knife ... Say it again ... a knife ... and this is a fork ... a fork [learners repeat] ... very good ... I'll put it here near the knife ... so a knife and a fork ... This is a spoon ... a spoon ... [learners repeat] very good ...

3 Ask the children to move some of the objects.

   ... Anong ... could you put the spoon in front of the fork? Thank you ... And now these are chopsticks ... Somsak ... can you put the chopsticks beside the knife? ... okay.

4 Ask the children to turn around and not to look at the table. Tell them that

▪ you are going to take away one of the things

■ when they turn around you want to see who will be the first to say what has been removed.

Now you all know what is on the table … Turn round and don't look … I'm going to take something away … no looking …okay … Now you can turn round again … and look carefully … What's missing? … What's missing? … Yes, Suwat … the salt … Very good … now … come up here.

5 The learner who says what has been removed takes the teacher's place and removes something from the table.

TEACHER *Suwat … you can take my place and decide what to take away the next time … Okay now … oh … here's the salt … You can put it back … and … you can begin now … What do you say first?*

SUWAT *(to the class) Turn around … don't look … (he takes something else away from the table and hides it) … Okay you can look now … What's missing?*

Variations

1 Use picture cards of any vocabulary topic learners are already familiar with.

2 Let a group of three or four learners leave the room. While they are outside the rest of the class hide two objects in different places. When the group comes in they have to say what is missing and try to find where the two objects are hidden.

Pronunciation

Practise the stress in these phrases and words:

TURN aROUND
You can LOOK NOW
a JUG of WATer

Remember that the letter 'k'

■ is not pronounced in the word **knife** /naif/
■ is pronounced at the end of the words **fork** and **chopstick**.

Follow-up suggestion

Ask your learners to draw a table set for a meal and draw or write what they would like to eat.

13 Pass the ball

LANGUAGE Phrases describing ten things using different colours and sizes, for example:

Set A	Set B
a small white cat	a big black cat
a big blue bird	a small green bird
a long pink scarf	a short green scarf
a small brown ball	a big orange ball
a small blue book	a big yellow book
a small purple flower	a big pink flower
a long blue pencil	a short red pencil
a small yellow cup	a big red cup
a big grey elephant	a small pink elephant
a small orange bear	a big brown bear

RESOURCES AND PREPARATION   A ball and some music.

Make two sets of ten pictures. You can use the samples in the Appendix or you can make your own.

TIME GUIDE   15 minutes.

Activity

1 Show your learners two drawings of a cat. Show them the big black cat first then show them the small white cat.

… Let's just look at this picture … Do you know what it is? … Yes, that's right. It's a cat … What colour is it? …. Yes … it's black … and now look at this picture … yes, it's another cat. And what colour is this cat ? Yes … it's white.

2 Now ask the class if the cat is big or small.

So … this is a black cat and this is a white cat … there's another difference … Is it a big black cat or a small black cat? Yes … that's right … so this a big black cat and … this is a small white cat …

Do this with all or some of the other picture cards

3 Ask your learners to make two circles with an equal number of children in each. Put 10 picture cards, Set A and Set B, upside down on the floor or on a table in the middle of each circle. Explain that they are going to play a game. The aim is for one group to correctly name all the 10 items first.

4 Stand outside the circles. Play some music or sing. Tell the children to pass the ball to the child next to them. When the music or singing stops the child with the ball picks up a card from the pile. He or she looks at the card, does not let anyone else see it, and asks the group 'What's on the card?' The others in the group have to guess what it is, the colour, and the size.

5   When the group guess correctly the learner shows the group the card and keeps it. Then the music or singing continues and the children pass the ball until it stops again. If the child with a card has the ball when the music stops, they pass it to the next learner. When every card has been picked up each learner shows his/her card to the class and says what it is.

Variations

1   Make big cards using ten

   ▪ actions like the ones used in 'Whispers' (Unit 21)
   ▪ positions, for example, 'behind the door', 'under the chair', 'beside the table', etc.

2   Instead of putting all the cards upside down in a pile put the cards in different places around the floor. Ask your learners to walk around in a circle. Play some music. When the music stops they have to stand beside one of the cards, pretend to be what it is on the card, and say what they are, for example, 'I'm a small yellow cup'.

Pronunciation

Practise the stress in:

a BIG BLACK CAT
a SMALL PURple FLOWer.

Follow-up suggestion

Link with your coursebook or a story where you can use similar descriptive phrases.

14 Simon says …

LANGUAGE   Movements, actions, and instructions, for example:

Put your hands on your head	Touch your elbow
Touch your ears	Touch your knee
Clap your hands	Take two steps forward
Stamp your feet	Sit down
Click your fingers	Stand still

RESOURCES AND PREPARATION   You need enough space inside the classroom or outside for all your learners to stand and face you.

Prepare a list of instructions for movements.

TIME GUIDE   10 minutes.

Activity

1 Stand in front of your learners and explain that you are going to call out some instructions. They

▪ have to listen very carefully
▪ have to do the movements
▪ should only move when you say 'Simon says'.

If you don't say 'Simon says', they must keep still.

2 Practise the activity with the class.

Okay … now I'm going to tell you what to do and remember only move when you hear 'Simon says' … If I don't say 'Simon says' … don't move … Are you ready? Right … Simon says put your hands up high … Very good … Simon says touch your ears … now … Touch your feet … oh oh … Some of you did it and I didn't say 'Simon says' … Okay that was just practice … Now let's start again …

3 If you do not say 'Simon says' and some children move, let them make a second group. The second group can continue to do the actions. You can make a third group if necessary. Making some extra groups gives your learners extra chances and it allows them to continue doing the actions. The aim is not to exclude children from the activity but to include as many as possible.

4 When there are three or four children left in the first group they can help you by calling out actions to other groups.

Variations

1 Use other key words instead of 'Simon says', for example, 'Please'.

2 With very big classes choose actions that children can do sitting down.

3 Think of actions that use real things (that everyone has!) and positions, for example, 'Find something red and put it on your chair'.

4 Instead of 'Simon says' do the activity by selecting children to move who are wearing certain clothes, for example, 'If you're wearing jeans stand beside the blackboard'.

Pronunciation

Practise the stress in these instructions:

PUT your HANDS on your HEAD
STAMP your FEET
CLICK your FINGers
TOUCH your ELbow
TOUCH your KNEE
STAND STILL

Follow-up suggestion

In teams of three or four let your learners think of six actions they would like the class to do. Help them make a list of these actions in English and use them the next time you play 'Simon says'.

15 What can you see?

LANGUAGE Revision of a vocabulary area that your learners are already familiar with, for example, animals and birds:

an elephant	a duck	a kangaroo
a mouse	a snake	a monkey
a giraffe	a hippo	a bear
a fish	a cat	a horse
a crocodile	a tiger	an octopus

The phrase, **I can see ...**

RESOURCES AND PREPARATION   Have a picture card for each item in the vocabulary set. There should be at least one card for each learner and one for the teacher.

TIME GUIDE   10 minutes.

Activity

1   Ask the children to make a circle. Put the picture cards where all the children can see them, for example, on the board or on a table or on the floor.

2   Tell the class they are going to remember and say the English names for all the animals on the picture cards. Say what is on each card as you put it down, for example, 'a mouse, a hippo, a tiger', etc. Take a card and say:

I can see a mouse.

3   Ask one of the class to repeat it.

TEACHER   *Now ... Lara can you repeat that please?*
LARA   *I can see a mouse.*

4   Give the card to Lara. Pick another card yourself and make a new sentence with the class.

TEACHER   *Good ... thank you ... now ... I am going to pick another card and let's see ... Will you all help me? ... Okay ... now ... I can see* [point to Lara's card] *a mouse and* [point to your card] *an elephant ... Now altogether ...*
CHILDREN *I can see a mouse and an elephant.*

5   Give the 'elephant' card to another learner. Tell the whole class to come to the board, choose a card, and go back to their circle. Tell them they are going to make longer sentences by adding their part each time. They should hide their picture until it is their turn.

TEACHER   *Okay ... now everyone take one card ... any card you like ... and go back to your circle* [children choose the cards]. *Let's see if we can remember all the animals ... Ready? ... We'll start again with you Lara.*
LARA   *I can see a mouse.*

TEACHER   *Good ... [point to Lorenzo] and Lorenzo ... Remember
          you have to add your word to Lara's [gesture to Lara's
          card].*

LORENZO   *I can see a mouse and an elephant [Lorenzo shows his
          card].*

TEACHER   *Very good. [pick another learner] Giuilia ... can you try?*

GIUILIA   *I can see a mouse, an elephant, and a fish [Giuilia shows
          her card].*

Go around the class with every learner adding to the sentence each
time until all the children have had a turn.

Variations

1   Use different verbs and situations, for example, 'I was in the
    supermarket and I bought ...'

2   Use any word sets that include vocabulary your learners are familiar
    with, for example:

- people (a farmer, a builder, a fireman), buildings (a post office, a
  school, a library), outside objects (a tree, a fence, a hill), etc.
- descriptive phrases; a blue van, a happy hippo, a monster with four
  eyes, etc.

Pronunciation

Practise the stress in these three syllable words:

CROCodile, ELephant, OCtopus.

Follow-up suggestion

Draw three animal houses on the board and ask the children to tell
you which animals could live together. Talk about why.

16 Odd one out

LANGUAGE	Topic vocabulary that your learners are already familiar with, for example, jobs, objects, animals, etc.
	Vocabulary for position, actions, descriptions, etc.
RESOURCES AND PREPARATION	Prepare several sets of cards with four picture cards in each set, for example: horse, giraffe, bird, and kangaroo. One card in the set should be obviously different from the others.
TIME GUIDE	10 minutes.

Activity

1 Put a set of picture cards on the board. Explain that all the pictures have something in common except one. That is the 'odd one out'.

> *Look at these pictures … a giraffe, a horse, a kangaroo … and this other picture … a bird … Which one is different? … Yes … the bird is different … These three animals can't fly … but … a bird … can fly … It has wings … So it's the odd one out … different from the others.*

2 Put up another set of pictures, for example, three pictures of flowers and a fish. Ask your learners to decide which one is the odd one out and explain why. Support them by asking questions and extending what they answer.

TEACHER	*Very good Michel … the fish … Yes … the fish is the odd one out … and why? Why is the fish the one out? … Where do we see fish?*
MICHEL	*… sea …*
TEACHER	*Yes … in the sea … and the flowers?*
MICHEL	*in garden …*
TEACHER	*In a garden yes … So we see flowers in a garden and fish in the sea … very good Michel …*

3 You can add more examples for your learners until they are used to doing the activity. Remember that there is often more than one reason why a picture is the odd one out. For example in the four pictures below a learner could say, 'there are two in the boat' or 'the people in the boat are sitting down' or 'she's the only girl'. These are all good reasons for choosing one of the pictures.

Variations

You can use:

- pictures of different actions, sizes, shapes, or colours
- word lists instead of pictures with similar differences: 'swimming', 'running', 'laughing', 'jumping'
- word lists with sound differences: 'mat', 'cat', 'jug', 'hat'
- phrases: 'See you tomorrow', 'Bye-bye', 'I'm sorry', 'So long'.

Pronunciation

Remember when you pronounce the word **different** you only say two syllables /ˈdɪfrənt/.

Follow-up suggestion

Let your learners work in groups and make their own sets of odd one out. They could cut out or draw pictures. Help them explain in English why one picture or word is the odd one out. Each group can ask the rest of the class to pick an odd one out. Collect the cards and keep them to use again.

17 What do I spy?

LANGUAGE Revision of colours, shapes, and sizes, and the names of things your learners use in the classroom, for example: **a pencil**, **a brush**, etc. Things in pictures around the classroom: **a star**, **the moon**, etc.

Rhyme: 'What do I spy?'

RESOURCES AND PREPARATION Everything you have in the classroom including the pictures on the walls. Be prepared to describe the size, shape, and colour of what your learners can see.

TIME GUIDE 10–15 minutes.

Activity

1 Tell your class that you are going to describe six different items in the room. You can tell them the size, shape, and colour of each item. They have to guess what you are describing. Say this short rhyme before you describe a new thing in the room:

What do I spy?
What do I spy?
Way down low
Or way up high.
Can you tell me
What I see?
It's near you
And it's near me.

…

It's in this room.
It's small and round and red.
What is it?

2 When your learners want to answer they should put up their hands.

Okay … do you know what I am describing? … Yes, Saori … you have your hand up … Yes … the pencil sharpener … on my desk … Very good.

3 When your learners have guessed your six items ask them to get into groups. Tell them to pick four things and prepare to answer questions from the other groups and to guess what the other groups' objects are.

4 When they are ready tell them that

■ each group has to say the rhyme before one learner says the clue
■ the team that guesses correctly gives the next description
■ if no one guesses a description from the size, shape, or colour, the team can give extra clues.

Variations

Ask your learners to give more clues in their first description. For example, they could say:

- what something is made of: 'It's made of wood', 'It's made of plastic', etc.
- what it is used for: 'You use it to drink water', 'You use it to rule the page', etc.
- what sound the name in English starts with: 'It starts with the sound "sh"'.

Pronunciation

Practise the stress pattern in the rhyme:

> WHAT do I SPY?
> WAY down LOW
> Or WAY up HIGH

And in descriptive phrases such as:

> It's ROUND and YELLow. (sun/moon)
> It's BIG and SQUARE and BROWN. (table)

Follow-up suggestion

Let your learners draw something they like and keep their drawings for the next time you do this activity.

18 Mix and match

LANGUAGE   Revision of vocabulary sets that your learners are familiar with.

Questions and answers: **Do you have the word … ? Have you got a picture of … ? Yes, I do. No, I don't.**

RESOURCES AND PREPARATION   Make packs with twelve matching picture cards and twelve word cards. Keep the picture and word cards separate.

There should be one pack for every four learners or in a very big class for every eight learners.

You can use all the same category (all animals) or mix the categories (animals, food, transport, parts of the body).

TIME GUIDE   20 minutes

Activity

1   Show your class some of the picture cards from one of the packs of cards. Ask the children if they can remember what they are.

> *Can you remember what this animal is called in English? … Yes … very good … a tiger … And this one … this isn't an animal … It's part of your body … yes … good … elbow … We have two elbows … Now this one is something we eat … yes … mango … very good …*

2   Put the picture cards on one side of the board.

3   Show your class the word cards one by one. Ask them to match the word cards with the picture cards on the board.

4   Tell your learners that they are going to play a card game in groups of three. The object of the game is to get four matching pairs of pictures and words.

5   Show them how to give out the twelve picture and twelve word cards so that no one sees what words or cards they have. They have to pick them up and look at them without letting the others see them.

6   Pick one learner in each group to start the game.

▪ The first learner asks the second learner on the left for a picture card or a word card that he/she needs to make a matching pair.

▪ If the second learner has this card, he/she hands it to the first learner and the first learner has to give the second learner a card – a word for a word and a picture for a picture.

▪ If a learner doesn't have the card then he/she answers 'No, I don't' and there is no exchange.

▪ The second learner then asks the third, the third asks the fourth, and so on. For example:

HIRO *Do you have a picture of a mango?*
MARI *Yes ... Here it is.*
HIRO *Thank you. Here's another picture card.*
MARI *Thank you ... Chie ... Do you have the word 'giraffe'?*
CHIE *Yes, I do. Here it is.*
MARI *Thank you ... Here's a word card.*
CHIE *Thank you ... Hiro ... Have you got a tiger?*
HIRO *... a tiger ... a picture?*
CHIE *Yes.*
HIRO *No, I don't.*

7 The game finishes when one learner has four pairs.

Variations

Put together packs of:

- picture cards with different coloured animals and objects like the cards used in 'Pass the ball' (Unit 13)
- picture cards with actions like the cards used in 'Whispers' (Unit 21).

Pronunciation

The letters 'd' and 'k' are not pronounced in san**d**wich /sænwitʃ/ and **k**nee /niː/.

The letter 'g' in ti**g**er, do**g**, and man**g**o is pronounced /g/ , in **g**iraffe it is pronounced /dʒ/.

Follow-up suggestion

Leave the picture cards on the tables and do an activity like 'What do I spy' (Unit 17).

19 Spot the difference

LANGUAGE　Household words the children are familar with.

Rooms and furniture: **a bedroom, a bed, a shelf, a small table, a dressing table.**

Personal possessions: **a lamp, curtains, a ball, a computer, a teddy, a pillow, a blanket, books, a TV, a mat, a blind, a toy ship.**

Phrases of position: **beside, opposite, under, next to.**

RESOURCES AND PREPARATION　Drawing materials: pencils, paper, etc.

Make a bigger drawing of the samples provided in the Appendix or make your own material. The copiable samples in the Appendix are:
- a bedroom with a window and furniture
- ten personal possessions.

TIME GUIDE　20–25 minutes

Activity

1 Put your drawing of the bedroom where everyone can see it.

2 Talk to your learners about the bedroom. Ask different learners to point to different objects.

   Okay … Luca … Point to the dressing table … Yes, that's right and … Rosa … Show me the mirror … Good … that's right.

3 Ask your learners to copy the drawing. Go around the classroom helping them and talking about their drawings.

4 When they are all finished explain that you are going to put up another big page with ten things you could find in a bedroom. Show them the ten items one by one. Ask them to put up their hands if they know what they are.

5 Tell them to copy any six things they like and put them anywhere in their bedroom drawing. They are not to let anyone else see their drawing.

   Okay … you can draw any six things and put them anywhere in your drawing … on top of the bed … or on the floor … beside the dressing table … under the window … [while you are speaking point to all the positions on the big drawing of the bedroom] anywhere you like … Okay …

6 When they have finished, make pairs so that children who were not beside one another in stage 5 are working together.

7 Without looking at one another's drawings and working in pairs each learner has to ask and answer questions to spot the differences between the two drawings.

MING *Do you have a bear?*
LI *Yes.*
MING *Where is it?*
LI *On the bed. How about you …?*
MING *Yes.*
LI *Where is it?*
MING *It's on the table … Do you …?*

Variation

Prepare other simple outlines: a classroom, a park, a zoo, a shop, etc. Draw or cut out pictures from magazines of ten extra items you usually find in these places and let your learners individually choose any six to add to their drawings.

Pronunciation

Practise the stress in these words and phrases:

PILLow, BLANKet, DRESSing TABle, CURtains, comPUter
TAKE your TIME
a BED with a PILLow and a BLANket
on the OPPosite WALL

Follow-up suggestion

Look at a picture storybook that your class are familiar with. Let them tell you where things are in the pictures.

20 Bingo

LANGUAGE A vocabulary set that your learners are familiar with, for example, occupations: **astronaut, baker, clown, cook, dentist, doctor, farmer, fireman/firewoman, footballer, mechanic, nurse, painter, teacher, photographer, pilot, policeman/policewoman, secretary, singer.**

RESOURCES AND PREPARATION Bingo design set out in a 3x3 grid like this one.

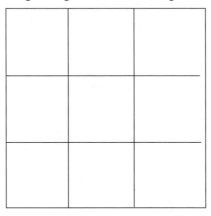

Picture cards of jobs you have used before that you can stick on the board.

TIME GUIDE 10–15 minutes

Activity

1 Show your learners about 20 job picture cards to help them remember the names for people's jobs. Show different parts of each picture first to see if your learners can recognise the occupations. As they call their answers out, write the names of the jobs on the board.

   Now … Who is this? … just look at the top of the picture … do you know who it is? Yes … yes it's a policeman … very good … Now I'll write 'policeman' here and put the picture beside the name …

2 Draw the bingo card grid with nine spaces on the other side of the board. Ask your learners to copy the grid onto a piece of paper.

   Now … over here I'm going to draw a bingo card … with nine spaces … I want you to copy this card … just like this …

3 Tell your learners to fill in the squares on their Bingo card with jobs from the list you have put on the board. They can choose any nine jobs they like.

4 When they have filled in all the spaces on their cards explain that

▪ you are going call out the names of nine jobs

▪ the class should listen carefully for the jobs on their cards

▪ when they hear them they should cover them with a small piece of paper

▪ the first person to cover all the jobs on his/her card calls out 'Bingo'

▪ he/she then reads out all the words again.

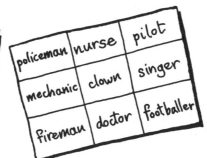

....

Variations

1 You can also use:

▪ colours – ask the learners to colour the squares and let each learner call out a colour

▪ the alphabet, dates, the time, feelings, any set of words from your coursebook

▪ descriptive phrases: a big black box, a small red ball, etc.

▪ vocabulary from a story, for example, from 'Little Red Riding Hood': wolf, granny, house, forest, woodcutter, flowers, basket, path, bed, glasses, teeth, mouth, etc.

2 Make the grid bigger, for example, a four square grid gives you sixteen squares.

....

Pronunciation

Practise the stress in these three syllable words:

poLICEman , phoTOGrapher
FOOTballer, SECretary

....

Follow-up suggestion

In groups let your learners help you to prepare more bingo cards using different topics.

21 Whispers

LANGUAGE Revision of vocabulary areas that your learners are already familiar with, for example, sports and leisure time activities: **running, swimming, playing tennis, listening to the radio, singing, playing basketball, watching TV, painting**.

Using **he**, **she**, and **they**.

RESOURCES AND PREPARATION Twenty pictures showing boys or girls on their own or together doing different activities. Use the pictures in the Appendix or prepare your own set of pictures.

Twenty written descriptions of each of the pictures: 'He's playing tennis', etc.

TIME GUIDE 15–20 minutes.

Activity

1 Put some pictures up on the board, for example, a boy playing tennis, a girl playing tennis, a boy and a girl singing. Explain the activity to your learners.

   Now look at the pictures on the board … and listen carefully … I'm going to describe one of them and you have to point to the one I'm describing … Okay … he's playing tennis … Yes, Luca … that's right … he's playing tennis … that's a boy … good.

2 Tell the class to get into groups. If there are twenty in your class, you could have four groups of five learners. Show the class how you want them to whisper a description by practising with two learners.

   Now get into groups of five. This time I'm going to describe a picture … but I'm going to whisper it … to Giuilia … and then I want you, Giuilia, to whisper what I said to Marco and he can point to the picture … Okay Giuilia … (whisper They're singing) …

3 Put a set of five written descriptions in a pile on the floor in front of each group and the matching set of pictures on the floor behind the groups.

4 Explain how to do the activity:
   - the first learner in each line picks up the first written description in their set
   - then he/she puts it back on the floor and whispers the description to the next learner in the line
   - each learner whispers the description to the next person until the last person in the line hears it.

The last learner in each line has to

- look at the pictures laid out on the floor at the back of the room
- find the picture that matches what he/she heard
- bring it up to the front
- check with the first learner and put it beside the written description.

5 This learner then becomes the first in the line and repeats the pattern in stage 4.

Variations

1 Use two sets of pictures, for example, pictures like the ones used in Unit 13 'Pass the ball'.

2 Use other pictures and phrases, for example: pictures from different stories and descriptions (the horse jumped into the river, the tiger swam quickly, etc.); pictures describing positions such as those on the dominoes set in the Appendix, for example, 'the pilot is standing in front of the plane', etc.

Pronunciation

Practise the stress patterns:

He's SWIMming
She's PLAYing TENnis
He's LIStening to the RAdio
She's RUNning
He's WATCHing TV
She's SINGing

Follow-up suggestion

In their groups help your learners make their own sets of picture cards with short descriptions. They can make a set for another group in the class to do the next time you do the activity.

22 Dominoes

LANGUAGE   Revision of vocabulary areas that your learners are familiar with, for example:

jug	hill	house	orange juice
cup	gate	carrot	mouse
pan	plane	sandwich	traffic lights
sausage	pilot	cake	car
wood	table	woman	tree

Prepositions: **on, in front of, between, in, behind, at, under, across, next to, up, down, above.**

RESOURCES AND PREPARATION   Copy the dominoes in the Appendix or make your own set. Prepare a set of 24 dominoes for every four learners in your class. In a big class every eight players could share a set with two learners playing together.

TIME GUIDE   15–20 minutes

Activity

1 Show your learners some picture and phrase dominoes.

2 Look at the domino with 'on the table' written on it. On the left side there is a picture of lots of trees and a person walking. Explain the activity to the class.

> *Okay ... can you all see this domino? Do you see what is written on it? 'On the table' but the picture shows a person walking in the wood. So the words don't match the picture. Now ... let's look at some more dominoes ... What will match the picture or the phrase? ... Here's a picture of a mouse on a table ... so we can put it next to 'on the table' ... Here we have the phrase 'in the wood' so we can put this beside the picture of the man in the wood ...*

3 Show your learners how

- to divide a set of dominoes between four giving six dominoes to each learner in the group
- they can place a card on either side of the first card so that either the phrase and picture match
- the game moves around the table in the same direction.

4 Give out a set of 24 cards to each group of four, six cards for each learner. They should place their cards face up on the table. Choose one learner at each table to begin.

5 The first learner puts down a card. The second learner checks to see if he/she can match the picture or the phrase and if possible puts down a matching phrase or picture. If learners cannot match a picture or phrase that is on the table, then

- they say 'Pass'
- it is the turn of the next learner
- they have to wait until it is their turn again.

6 In this way each player takes turns to put down a card that goes with a picture or a phrase. As the domino line gets longer they have to watch each end of the line. The learner who can put all his/her six cards down on the table wins! The group should help one another find a match for the remaining cards.

Variations

You can make domino sets using phrases that the children are familiar with, for example:

- sports and activities ('he's playing tennis', 'he's running', 'she's reading', etc.)
- transport ('by plane', 'on foot', 'by bus', etc.)
- faces and feelings ('she's happy', 'he's angry', etc.)

Pronunciation

Practise the stress in these prepositional phrases:

beTWEEN the HOUSes
beHIND the WALL
UNder the TABle
aCROSS the BRIDGE.

Follow-up suggestion

Show your learners how to make dominoes. Give them small cards with a dividing line. Let them work in groups to make dominoes to swap with other groups, for example animals, parts of the body, etc.

23 Making a word search puzzle

LANGUAGE Any vocabulary you want your learners to revise, for example, family words.

RESOURCES AND PREPARATION Prepare two large word searches on squared paper like these:

A

g	a	p	a	r	e	n	t	s	d	f	g
r	b	q	y	i	o	f	a	t	h	e	r
a	c	w	u	k	m	a	s	m	n	b	v
n	d	e	l	j	o	c	d	b	r	e	t
d	a	u	g	h	t	e	r	y	u	i	o
m	f	n	p	l	h	g	j	s	o	n	u
o	s	c	a	q	e	x	z	m	n	j	b
t	a	l	q	w	r	s	d	f	g	h	a
h	h	e	z	x	c	a	u	n	t	v	b
e	k	b	n	m	l	k	j	h	g	f	y
r	l	c	o	u	s	i	n	a	s	c	v

B

g		p	a	r	e	n	t	s			
r						f	a	t	h	e	r
a					m						
n					o						
d	a	u	g	h	t	e	r				
m		n			h			s	o	n	
o		c			e						b
t		l			r						a
h		e			a	u	n	t			b
e											y
r		c	o	u	s	i	n				

A and B are the same word search. Word search A shows the nine words hidden in all the extra letters. Word search B shows the nine family words: baby, mother, father, son, daughter, uncle, aunt, cousin, grandmother, and parents.

Bring in:
■ several smaller sheets of squared paper
■ some visual support, for example, pictures or photos of vocabulary your pupils know.

TIME GUIDE 20–25 minutes

Activity

1 Ask your learners to make a circle around the board and ask them to name the people in their families.

   Who do you have in your family, Andres? ... Yes ... your mother and father ... Good ... Now ... Isabel ... How many people do you have in your family?

2 Quickly revise all the family words that your learners know. Every time they remember a word write it on the board so they can read it as well.

3 Now show them word search A with family words and work with them to find the nine words hidden in it. Do this together in front of the board.

4 Show your learners word search B and tell them how you made the word search. Show them how words share the same letters or stand on their own.

Let's look at this word search without the extra letters. Do you see all the words? Do you see how you can put them on their own or you can use some letters in two words? ... Now ...

5 Divide the class into groups of three or four and give each group a topic, for example, food, colours, clothes, animals, etc. Give them some topic pictures/photos or cards for support, if you think they need them. Ask each group to make a word search puzzle for the others in the class. Give them some squared paper to work with. Tell them to

- think of the words first
- check how to spell the word
- put the words on the squared paper
- hide them with other letters.

6 Each learner in the group should write out the word search. Go around to each group to monitor and support. Check each word search for spelling before extra letters are added.

7 When the groups have finished, tell them to find someone from another group and swap their puzzles.

Variations

Let your learners decide how to design their own word searches. For example, they might like to make shapes like a house for furniture words or an airplane for travel words.

Pronunciation

Practise these stress patterns:

> **WHICH ones have you CHOsen?**
> **Do you KNOW how to SPELL that?**
> **Let's CHECK your SPELLing.**

Remember the silent letter in **knows** and the /tʃ/ sound in **chosen** and **check**.

Follow-up suggestion

Ask your learners to work in groups and think of six words that they find difficult to spell in English. Then they can ask the other groups to spell their words.

24 Crosswords

LANGUAGE Any vocabulary your class are familiar with, for example, clothes.

RESOURCES AND PREPARATION Prepare one crossword on a large piece of paper so that everyone in the class can see it. Here is a sample clothes crossword. The answers are at the end of the unit.

CLUES

Across:

3 It keeps your hand warm or safe.
4 It's warm and has sleeves and you wear it on the top part of your body.
6 You wear it on your foot inside your shoe.
8 It's a short coat with sleeves.

Down:

1 Trousers made of blue material.
2 It's like a small bag in your clothes for carrying things.
5 It has short sleeves and no collar.
7 You wear it on your head.

TIME GUIDE 10–15 minutes

....

Activity

1 Before you give your learners the sample crossword let them practise guessing a word. Tell them that you are going to describe something they know by giving them some clues.

I'm thinking about something. It's something you wear … It's long … and it keeps you warm … You wear it around your neck … or on your head … Do you know what it is? … Around your neck … Do you know? … Yes Ming … very good … a scarf … Yes … you're right …

2 Show your class the grid you have prepared on a big piece of paper. Show them the numbers in some of the boxes.

3 Tell them that they have to write the words in the boxes. The first letter of each word goes in a box with a number.

4 Show them how some of the words
- are written across the grid and some are written down
- share letters and this is an extra spelling clue.

5 Tell them they are going to have to think of eight clothes words. Divide them into pairs and tell them to help one another. Read out the clues one by one. When a pair guesses the correct answer, one of them can come to the front of the class and write it in the crossword.

Variation

Make a crossword puzzle about the characters and objects in a story including their actions and feelings.

Pronunciation

Practise the stress in these clues:

It KEEPs your HAND WARM or SAFE.
It's WARM and has SLEEVES and you WEAR it on the TOP part of your BOdy.
It has SHORT SLEEVES and NO COLLar.

Follow-up suggestion

Give each pair a topic and ask them to think of eight things they would put in a crossword. Help them to make simple clues and show them how to find good definitions in the dictionary. Show them how to use squared paper to make a crossword grid.

Answers to the 'Clothes' crossword
Across: 3 – glove, 4 – sweater, 6 – sock, 8 – jacket;
Down: 1 – jeans, 2 – pocket, 5 – T-shirt, 7 – hat.

25 Storytelling

This is a long unit and includes:

- 'The Magic Pencil', a sample story with drawings
- two lesson outlines.

Lesson One

LANGUAGE Focus on vocabulary:

- from the sample story
- that learners are familiar with
- that comes from their own contributions.

The story has been divided into twelve sections with drawings.

The Magic Pencil

1 Long ago there was a king. He was very mean. The people in his country were very poor.

2 The king had lots of money but he never helped anyone. He kept the money in the cellar of the castle. There was a big lock on the door and another one on the window.

3 A boy called Torna lived in the woods near the king's castle.

4 One day when he was coming home from school he saw a small wooden box under a big tree. Torna picked up the box and opened it. Inside there was a pencil and a piece of paper with a message:

I am made from a special tree
Pick me up and write with me
And if you are good and true
All your needs I'll give to you.

5   'Oh … all your needs …,' Torna said, 'and I am very hungry.' He picked up the pencil and wrote the word 'sandwich' in his notebook. Just as he finished the 'h' a big sandwich appeared beside him. Torna ate it. It was delicious.

6   Then Torna ran all the way home and said to his mother. 'What do you need?' 'We need food,' said his mother, and some new clothes.' Torna took out his notebook and wrote 'food'. As soon as he finished writing 'd' lots of food appeared in the kitchen. Then Torna wrote 'clothes'. As soon as he finished writing 's' new clothes appeared on the chairs in the kitchen. Torna's mother was amazed. He showed her the pencil and the message in the box. 'Well, you are good and true,' she said, 'and there are lots of poor people in our country who need things. You could help them.'

7   And Torna did. He helped a farmer. He asked him, 'What do you need?' And the farmer said 'We need a horse to help us on the farm'. So Torna wrote 'horse'. And as he finished the letter 'e' a horse appeared. The farmer was delighted.

8   He helped a painter. He asked him. 'What do you need?' The painter said, 'I need some paint.' So Torna wrote 'paint'. And as he finished the letter 't' 12 cans of paint appeared. The painter was so happy he went to work immediately. Torna helped everyone. But he remembered the message. He only wrote the words for what people really needed. Soon everyone was talking about the boy with the magic pencil.

9 But then the king heard about Torna. He asked him to come to the castle. 'Well,' said the king, 'I hear you can give people what they want.' 'No,' Torna said, 'the pencil gives people what they need. I only write the words.' 'Well,' said the king 'I need money. Write money.' 'You don't need money,' said Torna 'You have lots of money.' The king got very angry. He shouted at Torna. 'Give me your pencil. I can write it myself.' And the king grabbed the pencil. 'I want money,' he said, 'lots of money. I want mountains of money.' The king started to write 'mountains' … and when he got to the 's' the whole castle started to shake.

10 Torna ran out of the castle. But the king continued writing. The castle shook and shook. The walls began to crack. The floor began to break into small pieces and big mountains of earth pushed up through the floor.

11 All the money in the cellar flew up in the air. It was thrown all over the country. People thought it was raining money! The mountains went way up into the sky. And the king was never seen again.

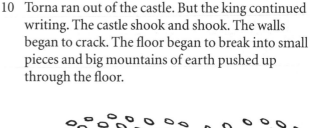

12 As for the pencil … Torna looked for it. He looked in the woods, in the rivers, in the towns. He looked everywhere. But the pencil had vanished. Maybe you will find it. If you do … be careful what you write!!

Mary Slattery

RESOURCES AND PREPARATION Before your lesson:

- Prepare some visuals – drawings, such as the ones that are used here, or your own drawings or collage pictures to go with the story. They need to be large enough for the whole class to see. If you make your own drawings, you can colour them and add several details that your learners are familiar with. You could also do this with collage pictures. Then you can talk about these extra things, for example, the rooms in the castle with furniture, animals in the wood near Torna's house, and so on.

- Pick out the vocabulary in the story that your learners are familiar with and the vocabulary that may be new. In this story you might have:

  Familiar vocabulary: pencil, money, king, castle, box, tree, food [examples in the picture], clothes [examples in the picture], horse, paint [different colours in the picture], write, give me, lots of, walls, floor, mountains, in the woods.

  New vocabulary: cellar, locks, good and true, needs, appeared, grabbed, shook, break into small pieces, crack, earth, thrown all over, vanished.

- Copy the twelve short sections of the story onto cards. Practise reading the cards that go with each picture so that you know the story very well. Then you will be able to tell it slowly using the cards as support while interacting with your learners at the same time. Remember to point to the people and objects, use gestures, movements, facial expressions, and change your voice to suit a character or a situation.

TIME GUIDE 30 minutes +

Lesson

1 Tell your class they are going to hear a story. Ask them to put their books, notebooks, etc. away before you begin. Tell them to listen carefully. If you think it might help the children enjoy the story more, re-arrange the class, for example, ask them to sit in a semi-circle away from their desks.

2 Let them predict what the story is about. For example, before you tell 'The Magic Pencil' story show the three main pictures, one by one: Torna, the King, and the pencil.

3 Tell the story. Use the pictures to help tell each section. Encourage your learners to talk about what they see in each picture. Ask them questions and make associations with what they know.

4 When words or phrases are new for your learners:

- repeat and rephrase the new words and phrases
- use the pictures for support and to help make the meaning clear.

> *'He kept the money in the cellar of his castle' ... Do you see the cellar? ... It's this room under the castle ... the cellar ... See this is all his money ... in the cellar ... under the castle ... Look ... the floor is covered with money ... and there's more here ... under the stairs ... There's money everywhere in the cellar ...*

5 Ask your learners to predict things.

> *'Oh ... all your needs ...' Torna said, 'and I am very hungry.' What do you think Torna wants to eat? ... an apple? ... ... some rice? ...*

6 If new vocabulary is non-visual, for example, 'appeared', 'grabbed', or 'shook', prepare to mime or demonstrate the meaning. Ask your learners to mime what happens at various times in the story.

> *'He saw a small wooden box under a big tree ...' Okay ... Can you see Torna under a big tree? Can you see him? ... Yes ... that's right Julie ... there's Torna and he's under that tree ... and he's picking up the box ... ... How would you pick up the box? ... slowly? ... or quickly? ... Show me how you would pick up the box ...*

7 For complex vocabulary, for example, the description 'good and true', talk to your learners about the meaning. Talk about Torna and how he helped people.

....

Pronunciation

Remember that the word **cellar** and **seller** are both pronounced /selə/ and the 't' in **castle** is not pronounced.

Practise the stress in these phrases:

> The CAStle SHOOK and SHOOK
> the WALLS beGAN to CRACK
> RAINing MONey.

....

Follow-up suggestion

After you have told the story you can ask your learners to draw and colour some extra pictures for the story. For example, you could ask them to draw and colour some of these: a room in Torna's house, his mother, any animals they have, the farmer's family, his farm, the kitchen in the castle, etc. Encourage your learners to do a different picture or part of a picture so they can all feel they have added to the story. Ask them for their own suggestions.

Lesson Two

LANGUAGE The main aim in this second lesson is to retell the story 'The Magic Pencil'. When retelling the story ask your learners to help so that they

- recall as much vocabulary as possible
- extend from their own additions to the story.

Young learners can remember whole phrases in context which gives them confidence and supports their own retelling of the story.

RESOURCES AND PREPARATION The pictures you used to tell the story for the first time.
Any pictures your learners made or drew and coloured at the end of lesson one.

TIME GUIDE 30 minutes +

Lesson

1 Ask your class if they remember 'The Magic Pencil'. Show them the first picture and ask them about it.

2 Put all the pictures on the floor or on a table. Tell the story again and include the pictures that your learners drew. As you tell the story ask them to put the pictures in the right order and put all the drawings on the walls around the room.

> *… He kept the money in the cellar of the castle … Yes … that's it … let's put it on the wall … Ken and Julie can you stick it on the wall for me, please? … Good … now let's look at the castle again … It's big … it has lots of rooms … What other rooms can you see in the castle? … Yes … there's another room … What room is it? …* [answer from the class] *that's right … It's the kitchen … Who did this drawing?* [answer from the class] *… You did, Ken … very good … Let's look at it … What can you see in the king's kitchen?*

3 When all the pictures are in the right order around the room use the activity 'Pass the ball' to go over the vocabulary again. Ask the whole class to stand in a circle. Play some music and pass a ball around. When the music stops, the person who has the ball with the help of their team has to do a task.

> *Okay … Ana has the ball … so … the yellow team … you can all help … show me the big lock on the window … very good … yes there's the lock and …*

or

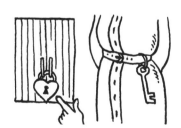

> *… Show me the key in the king's belt … Yes … that's right … There's the key … It's in his belt … Okay back to the circle.*

Go over all the vocabulary in the pictures in this way.

Variations

Dramatize the story as follows:

- Individual children can mime the actions as you read the story. Several children can mime one part – it helps if the children make and wear similar character masks. For example, one group can be Torna: one learner can be walking through the wood and find the pencil, another can arrive at his house and write 'food' and 'clothes', another can meet the farmer, etc.
- While the teacher reads the story and individual children act it out, the rest of the class can join in and add the dialogue, for example, 'I'm hungry ... ', 'What do you need?' – 'I need a horse', etc.'

Follow-up suggestions

1 Use other activities from this book. For example:

- play a version of 'Simon says ... ' that suits this story. If you say 'Torna says ... ', your learners do the action, but if you say 'The King says ... ', they should not move. Use instructions with vocabulary from the story, for example, 'Torna says pick up a pencil.' or 'The king says grab your pencil case.'
- ask your learners to fill out a 'Bingo' grid with any nine words from the story
- use any ten words in the story to make a word search puzzle for the class
- make a set of dominoes from words and phrases in the story
- use the activity 'Whispers' with pictures and phrases from the story.

2 Ask your learners what they would write if they had a magic pencil. Tell them to write their word on a small piece of paper. Put a big piece of coloured paper on the wall near part five of the story and tell the learners to stick their words on it.

Appendix

Here are the sample illustrations for units: 13, 19, 21, and 22.

Unit 13

Unit 19

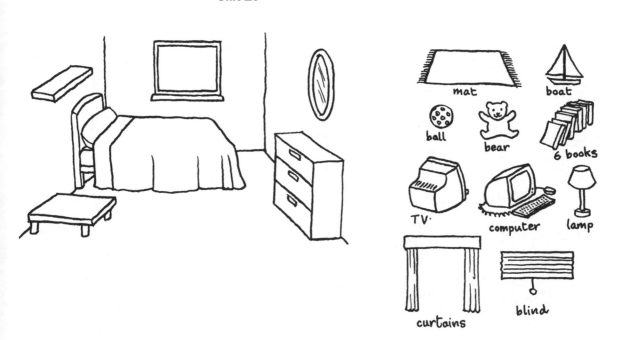

Unit 21

Unit 22

under the table	up the hill	at the traffic lights	down the hill
at the gate	in front of the jug	between the cups	in the pan
behind the house	next to the lion	in the car	under the tree
in front of the plane	in the house	next to the sandwich	in the box
under the umbrella	in the wood	between the houses	above the clouds
next to the cake	across the bridge	on the table	behind the wall